HOW TO VOTE TO SAVE THIS COUNTRY

An American Guide to Voting

Tony Maglione MD

createspace ™

CreateSpace is a DBA of On-Demand Publishing LLC,
part of the Amazon group of companies.

Printed in the United States of America

Library of Congress Control Number: 2010908327

ISBN 1452889007
ISBN 9781452889009

Dedicated to Thomas Paine, who had common sense.

Acknowledgments

Tony Maglione would like to thank his wife, Mindy, for all her contributions, including typing, editing, design, research, and support. She was invaluable to this book. A special thanks to Kristen Weaver for her help with design.

He also wishes to thank his parents, his brother, Massimo, as well as his sons, Christopher and Anthony, for their values and views that helped influence and reinforce his own beliefs.

Contents

Section II: <u>YES</u> Votes

Introduction

All elections are important, but the 2010 and 2012 elections may be the most important of our lifetime. We are at a turning point in our country's history. Every American should take each election at the local, state, and federal level seriously, and learn as much as he or she can about the candidates. However, the average American citizen does not have the time to evaluate all the candidates of an election fully. This book is an attempt to help you learn a time saving process that enables you to vote for candidates who are more suitable for the needs of the group they will serve.

To paraphrase a quote from Martin Luther King, Jr., the ultimate measure of a man is not where he stands in moments of comfort and convenience, but where he stands at times of challenge and controversy. The elections of 2010 and 2012 are moments of challenge and controversy, and all Americans need to stand and vote for what they believe in; that is, a candidate that most closely represents their values and can benefit not only their lives but also the lives of people around them now and for future generations.

One may ask, why I am writing this book at this time. Since the election and presidency of Barrack Obama (2008), it has become apparent that many of us who have been busy working and not directly involved in politics have become motivated to speak up at this time more than at any other time in the past. We are now witnessing a transformation of America that is leading us to more government involvement and control over our lives; that is, a socialist agenda similar to the European model and less concerned with our rising debt and liberal spending policies.

Recently, voting has become a popularity contest. A candidate has a better chance of success if the public perceives him or her as a pop-culture icon rather than the perception of his or her values and views on the direction of this country. Candidates are not chosen based on what they have actually accomplished in life, but rather on what they say they are planning to accomplish. Many people vote based on feelings without regard to facts available on the candidate. However, feelings can be falsely induced by the media or campaign propaganda. Facts stand on their own merit. People also tend to "go with the flow" of popularity in their social circles, such as friends and family and vote accordingly.

Why is my perspective unique? I believe my background allows a different perspective in that I was a son of immigrant parents living in New York, where my family and the majority of New Yorkers were liberal. I obtained my medical degree while living in Italy for five years, so I have the experience of living in a more socialist state with socialized medicine and more governmental control. Having grown up and worked in New York, I was exposed to a liberal philosophy. By also having lived and worked in the Southeastern U.S., I was subject to a part of the country that has a more conservative perspective. The south tends to be for more state rights and less big government oriented. Working as a doctor and running a business, as I did for a number of years, I experienced the impact of government bureaucracy first hand. Government bureaucracy complicated reimbursement or revenue from my patients, as well as payroll, benefits, and health care for my employees.

Aside from dealing with the bureaucracy, my profession as a doctor mandates a scientific approach to problems and their solutions. In taking care of patients, doctors have to take into account proven, successful results from prior studies and obtain useful information from patients. Thus, we use our knowledge and experience to help patients with their medical problems. We cannot spin or distort the facts to obtain a result. If we did, the patients would most likely be harmed, hurt, or would suffer. We should use these same principles when choosing a candidate so that we obtain real facts, data, and prior proven methods of success to prevent our country (who is now the patient in desperate need of good medicine) from harm or suffering. We must do this in spite of the bureaucracy.

As physicians, we are trained to ask questions constantly. We need to do this in order to understand the potential consequences of the answers at the moment and for the future. For example, if a patient comes to your office with chest pain and you, the doctor, dismiss it and do not treat the patient for a heart attack, the patient may survive that day but may suffer in the future from the heart damage caused by failure to treat the heart attack on the first day of symptoms. Therefore, you, the doctor, may ask yourself, do I want to take the chance of dismissing this chest pain as a non-critical condition? After asking the patient more questions and running some tests in the office, you will then equip yourself with enough information to make a good decision that will result in better care of the patient and a better outcome for the present as well as the future.

The average American citizen has never been taught to process information this way when it comes to choosing the correct candidate. However, we need to process information this way so that we can make more informed decisions on what will best suit our needs and the needs of our country. When caring for patients, the doctor is responsible for making the diagnosis, then explaining the diagnosis and treatment plan to the patient. The patient is then informed and consents to treatment. Similarly, the voting public needs to be well informed and then consent to the best candidates, who will lead the country to a healthier, more prosperous future.

The public should learn that if they continue to vote in the same pattern, their votes have consequences—similar to a patient who continues to smoke after a heart attack and, thus, has a greater chance of having another heart attack. If a voter continues to vote for the same type of candidate, there will be a greater chance of the same policies and practices we are seeing today. Politics will continue as usual without solving our serious issues, such as national

Tony Maglione MD

debt, education, immigration, the economy, and terrorism.

We need to use a more scientific method of asking questions and seeking not only which candidates are more suitable, but also which candidates are not suitable. Just like doctors know that certain decisions they make or treatments they recommend may be more harmful than others, some candidates may be more harmful than others. So knowing who not to vote for is as important as knowing who to vote for.

The list of people to vote for is shorter because they are more likely to have respect for the basic beliefs that are at the very foundation of our great nation. They share the spirit of our founding fathers—life, liberty, and the pursuit of happiness. They understand that sacrifices are necessary to keep those ideals at the forefront of what defines our nation.

The list of people not to vote for is a long one; I will specifically tell you, in my opinion, why, from both a practical and psychological perspective. These people will not lead this country to continued greatness, but rather they will help destroy it, while actually believing they are doing good for the country. This is because of the way they process information or were taught to think, which is usually a result of upbringing, profession, or social status. They are wired this way and unable to look outside of this box.

The most important issue to consider first is who not to vote for and why. Like when an employer reviews job applicants for a position, the employer needs to know which applicants or candidates can be eliminated first before considering which one is the best and should be hired.

Section I: **NO** Votes

Chapter 1

Attorneys

Most attorneys are trained to think their job is one in which winning a case is the ultimate goal. Although, even if they do a lousy job on the trial and lose, they still win by being paid. Even when they take cases on contingency, which means they are usually paid one-third plus expenses if they win and nothing if they lose, they usually take enough of these cases to offset the ones that they do lose, and they still get rewarded well financially.

They are taught to win the case as part of their profession. It does not matter if the defendant is guilty, because they can rationalize trying to win the case by saying everyone is entitled to the best defense. They are taught not to make any moral judgments since it is their job to defend even the guilty. When the cases do not settle and go to trial, one side wins and one side loses. On the average, attorneys lose trial cases 50 percent of the time.

The "win at all cost" guideline for their profession shows that they have to have very little or no moral base to guide them. For example, they would just as soon defend an innocent nun as a guilty killer if they were paid to do so. Also, in examples of divorce, if paid correctly, many would defend abusive husbands. In almost all cases of divorce, the lawyer is paid to prolong the case and encourage conflict amongst the spouses, which benefits the lawyers financially. When there is more conflict amongst spouses in divorce and more financial loss, the conflicting partners and their children lose; the only winners are the lawyers. This is also true of lawyers in Congress, since lawyers are generally paid by the hour, they are used to being compensated for talking or defending their arguments rather than for compromising or settling for what is best for all.

Of course, not all attorneys lack moral conviction, but the nature of their job usually doesn't question any moral base, such as is the defendant really guilty? In many cases, they follow the law, but the law can be interpreted in different ways, and killers can be released through loopholes or problems with the legal process, such as evidence obtained through improper channels. In this case, the lawyer and murderer win, but society loses.

These are reasons why attorneys, in general, are not good candidates. Their profession does not embrace good, core moral values. Take for instance malpractice attorneys. In many cases, they are considered ambulance chasers looking for accidents they can profit from, or they run advertisements to solicit people who perceive that they have been harmed by a doctor, product, or drug. There should be a system of checks and balances that protects against wrong doings by manufacturers or health care providers, but there isn't. And, while attorneys' motivations may seem to be doing good and protecting the public, since the judgments are usually of high monetary rewards, most of the time, it is the attorney that mainly profits from these cases.

With respect to malpractice cases, attorneys often take the cases that evoke the most sympathy and grant the highest rewards, such as maternity suits where babies are born with abnormalities. These abnormalities may have nothing to do with the delivery or care provided by the doctor or hospitals. Many times the abnormality is due to genetics or acts of nature. However, the malpractice attorney will display the baby or child's handicap, which causes a jury to consider the case on emotions instead of facts. John Edwards practiced law in North Carolina this way, and we certainly now know that he is not one we can trust. These cases, disguised as helping the public, often create real public safety and health concerns. Because of the highly increased risk of malpractice suits in obstetrics, obstetricians are now in short supply in several states such as Pennsylvania, Florida, and Arizona, which has placed more Americans and their unborn children at risk. In Los Angeles, where malpractice reforms are in place, an obstetrician pays about $63,000 a year for malpractice insurance. That same obstetrician in Miami, with no reforms in place, pays $277,000.

Trial attorneys are big supporters of Obama. Why? Malpractice reform is not mentioned in the Healthcare and Education Affordability Reconciliation Act of 2010. For malpractice attorneys, the health care reform bill did not subject them to any sacrifices or loss of potential income. Without considering malpractice reform in the bill, attorneys stand to continue benefiting, while citizens, hospitals, doctors, and the insurance companies bear all the loss and sacrifice. The attorneys have nothing to lose. They can still sue doctors and hospitals and go after huge financial rewards for pain and suffering. How does this help the majority, when malpractice attorneys make up less than one in several thousand

U.S. citizens?

Common sense would dictate that if you want to control rising costs in health care, you would need to look at the costs in every aspect, not just insurance premiums and physician and hospital fees. This means addressing tort reform, mainly by capping pain and suffering settlements, as has been done in many states, such as Texas and California. Tort reform should also include removing the jury system and substituting a panel comprised of medical and legal experts, such as doctors and judges. These experts are in a better position to determine guilt or innocence. They would also make more appropriate financial rewards in malpractice cases as they are unbiased by emotional aspects. This would also decrease health care costs by eliminating the need for lengthy malpractice trials. In addition, tort reform would have a more positive affect on the way physicians practice by decreasing defensive medicine and the utilization of expensive technology, hence lowering health care costs.

It is the nature of the profession that allows attorneys to be more interested in the result than the process—such as winning a case at all costs versus arriving at the truth and more appropriate justice being served. Also because of the nature of their profession, they can switch sides easily, defending innocent or guilty people. This leads to an inability to differentiate between what is truly right and what is truly wrong. Most Americans believe that it is wrong to place an innocent person in jail and right to incarcerate a guilty person. Attorneys can just as easily defend a killer one day and the next day defend an innocent by-stander.

Therefore, why vote for someone who thinks and processes like an attorney? They can easily switch sides if it benefits them. Remember, their goal is to win and defend at all cost, but not to always do what is right. A recent prime example is Arlen Specter, the senator from Pennsylvania, who for many years had a party affiliation with Republicans and shared many of their values, but when those values no longer benefited him, he switched parties in an attempt to win reelection.

Today's Congress consists of too many attorneys. As of 2009, 54 percent of the Senate and 36 percent of the House were lawyers. This means that lawyers comprise about 40 percent (211 out of 535) of the legislative branch of our country, while lawyers comprise less than ½ of 1 percent of the U.S. population.

Looking at the recent past, before entering politics, Ronald Reagan was an actor, not an attorney. George W. Bush was a successful businessman. George H. Bush was a successful oil businessman. Dwight Eisenhower was an accomplished military leader. John F. Kennedy, after his naval service, went into Congress and was not a lawyer. Lyndon B. Johnson was a teacher. Clinton, who we know lied to the American people by pointing his finger and stating, "I did not have sexual relations with that woman," went to Yale Law School. Barrack Obama who promised a transparent government as well as no tax increases to those making less than $250,000 went to Harvard Law School. Gerald Ford was an attorney, who pardoned Nixon, also an attorney, for lying to the American public during Watergate. Remember, President Nixon was impeached by Congress and had to resign, while Clinton was impeached by the House of Representatives for lying under oath. Jimmy Carter was a peanut farmer; I don't want to insult any peanut farmers, but we Americans would have been better served had he remained a peanut farmer.

The problem is not the process of becoming an attorney; it is the practice of law in this country once one is an attorney. It is not the profession that is the problem; it is how attorneys think or rationalize their beliefs that are the problem. There is less concern about the facts or truth because they can argue either side well, and if they become politicians, they know how to circumvent or spin issues or legislation in order to promote their party's or their own agenda.

Attorneys do not like to lose, so they usually try to win one way or another. This is why, as politicians, if they are not winning a debate or issue by consensus, they will change or manipulate the rules to "win," as they did with the healthcare reform legislative process. They considered the use of reconciliation, because they had lost their super majority (60 votes) in the Senate after the Brown election in Massachusetts. Instead, the House of Representatives in March, 2010 amended the original Senate version of healthcare reform passed in December, 2009 to avoid another Senate vote. This is an example of circumventing or manipulating our legislative process in order to pass their desired agenda.

Due to the large number of lawyers in Congress, we see enormous bills, often consisting of thousands of pages, filled with legal terminology that no one can understand. We often hear that Congress doesn't even read these bills; this probably explains many things. We need to endorse "simplification attorneys" a new law practice that simplifies legislation so that all Americans can understand. In other words, what we really need are attorneys that help simplify the existing laws. The current laws are so complicated; most attorneys cannot understand them, let alone the average American citizen. These laws are ambiguous and can be interpreted in several ways—such as the IRS tax code, which helps those familiar with manipulating the system benefit from its complexity, while the average, honest American citizen loses. Secretary of the Treasury Geithner used the "complicated tax code" as an excuse for not paying his very own taxes.

Since many attorneys value winning over all else, they may overlook the truth and conveniently change their position to reach their goal. In general, one should not vote for attorneys because the truth for them is subjective. This is why they feel it is okay to fight to win rather than get to the truth. Also, they justify that as long as it is legal, they will use whatever means possible to win. This may be helpful in negotiating with an adversary, but not as a moral leader of our country. Many times attorneys win by twisting or exaggerating facts or events or by suppressing evidence. Even if the truth is evident, they may still try to win on a technicality.

This goal is, many times, self-serving and not in the best interest of most Americans. Therefore, they are on the list of "who not to vote for."

Chapter 2

Bureaucrats

As a whole, bureaucrats are not qualified to hold public office. A bureaucrat is one who works for the government as a government official. For the sake of this discussion, I am not including those who work in our defense at all levels of government, such as military, law enforcement, CIA, FBI, and firefighters. Bureaucratic officials are less accountable for their job performance and usually have job security since it is very difficult to be removed or fired. Bureaucrats also tend to over-step or abuse their positions of power. There are many examples of this; for instance, the IRS is a government agency that, when one is audited, assumes guilt until you have proven your innocence. This is in direct contradiction to our legal system, which presumes innocence until proven guilty. Their approach is a strong-arm tactic, where the threat is, "You pay now or go to jail." Of course, wealthier people who have enough income can defend themselves, whereas middle class people without enough financial resources end up having to pay or go into financial ruin. Those within the system are not held to the same standards and do not follow the same rules as the general public. For instance, when it was discovered that Tim Geithner did not pay all of his taxes, he was rewarded by becoming the Treasurer of the United States, thus in charge of the IRS.

Bureaucrats do not look at their work as a profession, but rather as a job. They usually do as little as necessary to get by and make it through the day. This creates a less efficient and more costly agency. For example, many of the officials in charge of running government agencies such as the post office, Medicare/Medicaid, and Social Security usually do not care about the purchasing costs of supplies and items, or their budget. The way that they think and process causes them to approach their work without regard to any personal responsibility or accountability. Because their jobs are generally protected, even if their departments have tremendous monetary loses and waste, they feel no sense of responsibility, since there is a general belief by bureaucrats that the money will keep coming. Of course, that money is coming from the taxpayer, the American citizen.

When JFK was president, he supported government workers to unionize. Over time, this helped protect these workers from being removed from their positions, even if their departments were determined to be over budget and full of waste.

What the government worker fails to recognize is that the government makes no money. The money in government that pays their salary comes from the taxpayer, who has a right not to pay for wasted motion and limited effort.

There is currently a move by liberal progressives to have our country become more like the European model. Having lived in Italy for five years, I can attest to how absurd the bureaucracy has become in many aspects of the average Italian citizen's life. In Italy, for example, one had to stand in line with a form that needed a special stamp in order to obtain the proper form to ask for a specific service, such as a university transcript. Needless to say, this involved duplication of time spent in line, but this could have been done more simply and efficiently without the stamp or without having to stand in line at all. Who knows how much extra these unnecessary steps cost the individual, but at least the people who made the stamps profited, and another government job was created for each stamper.

A similar example in our country is the speed in which you can renew your driver's license at the Division of Motor Vehicles. Would anyone consider this an example of an efficiently run department?

The government's ineptitude is seen in health care with the Veteran's Administration (VA). For veterans who are healthy, it serves as an adequate health care system for screenings—yearly medical exams and blood work. For those veterans that have chronic illnesses and are aging, the VA is failing in delivering optimal health care. I have witnessed the VA becoming increasingly more bureaucratic and this has had a negative effect on the health care rendered to these veterans.

In an attempt to save the department money, the VA only offers generic medications, which are usually less effective than brand name medications. Generic medicines are older medications that have lost their patent after being on the market for ten to fifteen years. The newer, most recently studied, and more effective medications, in many cases, are not available to our veterans. The veterans of our country receive the same generic medications that the inmates in our prison system receive. It is a sad testament to our nation that the very people who defended our freedom and risked their lives now have substandard and often inadequate health care.

As a cardiologist, I am often consulted to see veterans with heart disease. In some cases, the veteran has conditions that do not require immediate hospitalization or are non-emergencies. Although, they do require a work-up with diagnostic testing, such as stress testing and heart catheterizations in a timely manner, this usually means within a week or two. However, as a cardiologist, I cannot even do the simplest diagnostic test, such as an EKG in the office, let alone more sophisticated tests that need to be done quickly, without prior authorization from the VA. I have to fill out a form that goes back to the VA for approval of the procedures recommended, but it may take months before I get approval or the VA arranges for their own doctors to perform the procedure. As a cardiologist, I feel like I'm back in Italy standing in line for the proper stamp of approval for my patient.

The same bureaucrats at the VA do not realize or care that

veterans with serious heart conditions cannot wait for several months, and often end up at the emergency room of non-VA hospitals. Conditions such as chest pain may lead to heart attacks and/or death if not addressed in a timely fashion. These non-VA hospitals either try to get approval for care of the veteran or try to transfer the veteran to one of the VA hospitals. Many times, it is nighttime or the weekend, and no one is available for this approval; thus, the non-VA hospital has to take care of the emergency in order to care for the veteran properly. Without approval, the hospital and doctors who care for the veteran must absorb all the costs. This may save the initial cost to the VA by having someone else foot the bill, but in the long run, the patient's health status is placed in danger and the overall health costs, when treated as an emergency, increases.

Bureaucrats are responsible for more waste than in the private sector for the reasons mentioned above. They are not accountable for balancing the books and, therefore, do not worry about whether things cost more than anticipated, because the money keeps coming from sources within government. There is no fiscal restraint to their spending and waste. For example, if a bureaucrat spends over budget, they request a bigger budget for the next year. They are not concerned about the debt they have accrued. How many parents would give their teenager another credit card if the teen had already maxed out the first card and is in debt? Those that do, act as irresponsibly as our government when continuing to provide monies to departments that continue to have waste and failed budgets.

Another example of bureaucratic inefficiency and waste is in the government's approach to identifying health care fraud. Instead of going after medical providers who charge for a service or procedure they do not perform, the government has developed reviewers that audit the doctors' documentation in patients' charts for up to three years prior. They deem that a fraudulent act is committed when there is an omission of one word or sentence in the doctor's documentation of a patient's chart. Any omission of the documentation they require in a patient's record usually results in fining the doctor. The fine requires the doctor to return payment of the patient's visit or procedure. For example, if a patient is having a heart attack and the doctor, who is naturally more concerned with saving the patient's life and does that quickly and successfully, did not have time to ask the patient and document whether he/she had certain symptoms that did not pertain to having a heart attack, he or she may have to give back the payment for services rendered. These same bureaucrats can then unfairly review as few as twenty charts of this doctor, and if they find (what they consider) missing documentation on half of them, they will fine the doctor for half of the patient encounters that he or she submitted claims for that entire year. For instance, if the doctor saw two hundred patients in the hospital that year, he/she would be fined for one hundred patients, meaning he/she will have to return payment for one hundred patient visits, or half the money earned in the hospital that year.

This way of confronting perceived fraud does not improve health care and does not lower costs because it does not address quality issues and the actual costs of patient care. It instead focuses the attention away from real medical fraud, which requires more effort by the bureaucrats to find doctors who do defraud the system intentionally by charging for services never provided. It is easier for these same bureaucrats to go after easy money by finding honest omissions in chart documentation. This, in effect, fines many well-intentioned and hard working doctors that cared for their patients' appropriately. This line of thinking by the bureaucrats to obtain monies by fining doctors on technicalities, while telling the public that they are working hard to decrease fraud in health care, is similar to how a lawyer thinks by using a technicality to win a case.

To anyone with common sense, it is easy to see that the real fraud is committed by the bureaucrats for not going after the actual fraudulent people in health care. Bureaucrats tend to be more interested in their process of following steps or written rules and regulations regardless of whether this actually helps solve the problem. This health care example is one that does not begin to solve the fraud in health care, diminish its cost, or benefit the patient in any way.

In spite of the above, the government has the capacity to do some things well. They are needed as safeguards in protecting Americans when private industry acts with greed and self interest and takes advantage of the public. Enforcement of current regulations in Wall Street and with bank industries is needed to keep our economy strong. Unfortunately, the government is not doing a good job safeguarding itself from its own greed and self interest and, therefore, cannot adequately safeguard others such as the private industry.

As such, bureaucrats cannot be trusted to do what is in the best interest of most Americans. They have little accountability and appear to address their own needs first by preserving their jobs and pensions and maintaining their power base. This is why they are on the "who not to vote for" list.

Chapter 3

Politicians

Politicians are included in the "who not to vote for" for several reasons. Even though many, initially, have good intentions and feel a need to serve, eventually they become victims of their own need for power and get entrapped by the position. Over time, the need for reelection and maintaining their power base becomes more important than their principles. Many politicians are attorneys (approximately 40%) and look at issues the same way attorneys look at issues. Many times, politicians argue one side only to switch when this argument suits their needs at the time. For example, many Democrats such as Harry Reid and then Senator Obama disagreed with using reconciliation for spending bills when George W. Bush was president. But when it was needed for the Democrats to pass their health care agenda in 2010, they were both vehemently in favor of reconciliation. This is not only hypocritical, but also disingenuous.

Politicians are really only accountable at election time. Even though they may have broken numerous pledges, the power of their position and the connections they have made, enable them to obtain enough exposure and money to be reelected. Incumbents in the House of Representatives have won reelection over 90 percent of the time in the last twenty years, and over 80 percent in the Senate.

Many politicians tend to make special deals while in office, which benefits them more than their constituency. We all know of Congress voting late at night for their pay raises. Also, there are many examples of wasteful pork added to bills that benefit individual politicians and few constituents. Usually, the pork is added to help the politician get reelected. It is obvious to anyone with common sense and his or her priorities in order that so called "pork" should be voted on its own merits rather than attached to an existing bill.

When discussing major legislation such as war or domestic issues such as health care, many politicians feel entitled to receive deals in order to give their support to the bill. This shows that politicians are not willing to vote on the merits of the bill itself. It shows that they can be bought for a vote. For example, recently,

Ben Nelson, the senator from Nebraska, received a special deal for only his state when he changed his vote to pass the Senate version of the health care bill in December, 2009. While this may benefit some people in Nebraska, this is unfair to the rest of the people in the U.S. This demonstrates a lack of moral character, where a U.S. Senator, voting on a national issue such as health care, only considered his state. Are we not fifty states of Americans?

It is not just this one senator. Today's Democrats represent a party that believes in bigger government as its main objective. This inevitably leads to more spending, increased debts, more taxes, and more government take over of the private sector. The government is the biggest bureaucracy. As stated previously, bureaucracy only creates waste and fraud and is inefficient. In general, most politicians act like bureaucrats where they do not hold themselves to any budget. It is the taxpayers' money that they feel free to spend and spend. Unless there are laws to restrict their habits, which means putting restraints on their spending (such as a balanced budget), politicians will naturally continue to spend and most likely waste more of our money placing today's and future generations in financial chaos.

Furthermore, politicians generally do not learn from their mistakes and tend to repeat them. For example, when there were problems with the quality of our education—lower nationalized scores on subjects compared to other nations—despite putting more money into the same methodology of teaching, the response was to continue putting more money into that methodology, resulting in no improvement in nationalized test scores. It is apparent that the money would have been better spent in newer more innovative programs that were tested in certain locations. The programs that were successful in raising test scores should then be the ones chosen to implement and invest in. Rather, these politicians, mainly for political reasons, continue to put money into programs that fail. How does this help the American student?

As a cardiologist, I teach prevention, such as lifestyle changes that will decrease the chances of heart disease. This is preventative medicine. However, our politicians almost always react, and are not proactive. To be a good physician and a good legislator, one needs to do both, having effective strategies to prevent problems and to react to problems.

After serving for a number of years, it does not matter which political party is in office. The natural tendency for most politicians is to maintain their elected position and position of power, not to serve the people. This is why there should be term limits. No one should be elected to office for more than twelve years in his or her lifetime so that the temptation of corruption (deal making) and the "subconscious" need to maintain power is eliminated. Politicians who feel the need to serve more than twelve years may act as consultants to candidates they support. Therefore, when in doubt, vote against the incumbent who has been in office for many years. They are more prone to want to keep the power of their office than to want to serve their constituents.

Our founding fathers felt it is best to serve for a short period of time rather than as a life long profession. George Washington did not seek a third term and Jefferson wrote in 1807 that a constitutional amendment should be made to limit one's time in office.

Therefore, we should not vote for politicians who do not adhere to their pledges, such as promising transparency or promising not to raise taxes. We should not vote for politicians that need special deals in order to obtain their vote on a bill. We should not vote for politicians who say one thing one election cycle, and then the total opposite on the next election cycle. We should not vote for politicians who believe that remaining in office is the ultimate goal. We should not vote for politicians who change their party affiliation after being voted into office.

We should vote for politicians that support a law that they cannot change their party affiliation after being voted into office. We should vote for politicians that support term limits, not just for others but also themselves. We should support politicians that will not add pork or sign bills that have pork in them. We should vote for politicians that believe in a balanced budget and not increasing the debt. We should vote for politicians that not only worry about their budget from year to year (as American families have to do), but also worry about their budget and financial situation ten to twenty years into the future.

Chapter 4

Lobbyists

Lobbyists are a group of people who try to persuade politicians to vote in a particular way. Many are former politicians themselves who try to influence government decisions through their previous connections with individual politicians currently in office. These lobbyists are usually very well paid and represent a special interest group, such as trial lawyers, insurance companies, labor unions, corporations, pharmaceutical companies, and the like. The lobbyist advocates for that group by trying to influence the leaders in Congress to vote a certain way for a particular bill. The ability to lobby the government is protected by the first amendment of the Constitution with the right to petition.

Generally, lobbyists act in a self-serving manner because they only represent one point of view and are not looking at the whole picture or what might possibly be in the best interest of most American citizens. For example, in the medical field as a doctor,

I have dealt with many pharmaceutical representatives trying to lobby for doctors to use their medications for a particular illness, such as high blood pressure. There are many high blood pressure medicines on the market and as doctors, we have to consider the whole picture when prescribing a blood pressure medicine. The whole picture includes how well the medicine works, how well it will work for that particular patient, side effects, availability of the medication through the patient's insurance, and cost to the patient.

Pharmaceutical companies must invest a lot of money into the research for developing a certain medication, which usually is at least several hundred million dollars. When the FDA approves a drug, the pharmaceutical company tries to promote or lobby for this medicine as a new medication for blood pressure that is better than the other drugs for high blood pressure on the market. This results in an aggressive lobbying for doctors to use this medication because they are trying to recoup their initial investment from developing this drug. Before prescribing it, doctors like to have as much proven science and clinical research possible, showing that a particular medication is better when compared to others. Many times these new drugs do not have the same number of research studies as the older drugs do, because they are obviously new to the market. The pharmaceutical representative, because it is in his or her interest, has to believe that the medication is better than the others, even if studies do not yet prove that. Therefore, he or she tries to convince doctors that this medication is better and should be their drug of choice for high blood pressure.

In general, most doctors still rely on proven scientific research rather than a hard sell. This is because they are more interested in what medication will help the patient than in pleasing the pharmaceutical representative. Even though pharmaceutical representatives may bring the doctor lunch or take them to dinner for a lecture to learn about their drugs, this enticement usually does not cause the doctor to prescribe that medicine. If a doctor simply followed the recommendations of the pharmaceutical representative or was influenced by a free meal, and later studies proved that the new drug being lobbied was not as good as expected, the doctor's actions would not have been in the best interest of the patient.

This is not the case in Washington, D.C. In general, many of our elected officials will be swayed by the lobbyists or accept the perks offered by the lobbyist and, thereby, do what is best for their own interests instead of what is best for the American citizen. Trial lawyers successfully lobbied Congress to keep tort reform out of the Healthcare and Education Affordability Reconciliation Act of 2010. Trial lawyers are major contributors to the politicians who voted for this health care reform bill, which did not include any meaningful tort reform. Anyone involved with health care knows that in order to reform health care, one has to look at all the components of cost, such as insurance premiums, hospital charges, doctor's fees, and especially issues such as the cost of defensive medicine. Defensive medicine is practiced by doctors due to the lack of adequate tort reform, which was completely ignored by both houses of Congress due to successful lobbying by trial lawyers.

Many lobbyists think like lawyers. They are beholding to whoever pays them and, therefore, money, not principles, dictates their loyalty. Lobbyists have too much influence, especially when the lobbyists are former politicians with connections and ties with current politicians. Deals are made to aid the politicians and the lobbyists' interests—they tend to scratch each others' backs. If a politician votes in favor of the lobbyist's employer, the politician can then depend on continued financial backing at the time of his or her next election.

Therefore, lobbyists and any candidate they support are not to be trusted; they are on the "who not to vote for" list.

Chapter 5

Union Leaders

U nion Leaders, many years ago, were needed to stem some of the abuses by employers in the work place. Nowadays, there are so many government regulations protecting the worker, the union leader's role has evolved into one that is more like an agent for the worker rather than his/her protector as they were in the past. Union leaders act like agents (like for athletes or celebrities) and try to get the best deal in terms of salary and benefits for the workers. They do this without regard to how this affects the overall cost and productivity of the entire company. For example, with General Motors in Detroit, there was strong union leadership and the workers got much higher salaries and better benefits at GM than the other car companies. Other car companies in the US had employees making $20 to $30 less an hour in pay and benefits. These other car companies have remained a viable business, while GM required bail out money, loans, and federal intervention (by taking over a majority of the company's stocks) in order to remain solvent as a company. Union leaders may be popular with the workers they represent for a while, but many union workers lost their jobs as a result of downsizing due to economic hardships at GM. The role of the union leader, as an agent for the workers, is not a good long-term strategy to keep American workers employed. Union leaders have become like the bosses of old that abused their employees. The union leaders, by their unreasonable and over-priced negotiated demands, are now the abusers, killing American productivity and resulting in more loss of jobs.

Union leaders also have another agenda in mind, which is to socialize the work force and make all American workers essentially receive similar pay and benefits. The SEIC, who has Andrew Stern as its most public leader, is trying to increase the number of unions in this country by his connection with the White House. The SEIC was a big contributor to the Obama presidential election and Andrew Stern is one of the most frequent visitors to the White House on record.

The goal is to increase the size of government, which allows two things to happen: (1) unionization of its workers and (2) either having the government take over much of the private economic sector (such as health care, banks, Wall Street, car companies) or to legislating easier ways for unions to get into the private sector. These methods will allow more unionization of more American workers. When union leaders have more power and control, they will essentially be like bureaucratic leaders, and the workers will be less productive and less accountable, and it will be difficult for substandard workers to be fired. This will cost the American people more money by increased waste in government spending.

Therefore, union leaders and any candidate they support are not to be trusted, and are on the "who not to vote for" list.

Chapter 6

Mainstream Media Supported Candidates

The media is supposed to be paid to do their jobs, which is to get at the truth and expose fraud, and to keep government honest. They are supposed to be vigilant and serve as the safeguards of the American constitution by looking out for American citizens' interests. However, the majority of the media, who I will refer to as the mainstream media, does not do this job well, and is not trustworthy. The majority of the media (over 80%) vote for Democrats or are to the left themselves. They should not let their personal political beliefs influence their jobs. But recently, they have shown no objectively, and have become a mouthpiece for the Democratic Party.

In the past, the media would do the work necessary to validate their facts prior to their story, now it appears they are too lazy to put in the time necessary to check their sources and go after the truth. Instead, they let their personal beliefs dictate how they will report a story. For example, in the 1970s, Bernstein and Woodward were journalistic watchdogs who spent the time and resources necessary to follow the leads and eventually the facts exposing the Watergate scandal.

Today, our culture has become more image oriented rather than achievement oriented. The media helps prop up the importance of Hollywood stars and athletes as well as their own perceived importance or fame. As with lawyers, lobbyists, and union leaders, this tends to be self-serving. The media should be reporting facts and letting the public decide what to think based upon the facts reported. Instead, the media wants to tell you what you should think and which candidate is worthy of consideration. It is easier for them to pontificate their own views than to recount the facts objectively.

The media is much like trial attorneys, politicians, and lobbyist who spin the truth or ignore the truth for their own personal, political agenda. For example, the mainstream media would not report on the ACORN scandal because it supported its political agenda. The wrong doings of ACORN were not of concern to the mainstream media. It took a political commentator, like

Glenn Beck, (who is not a journalist) to expose the truth and bring the story to the American people.

Therefore, the media as a whole cannot be trusted. They do not ask the right questions. They are more concerned with whether an issue helps Democrats or Republicans and less concerned with whether it helps Americans. This is why the candidates supported by the mainstream media are ones that you should not vote for. These candidates tend to want big government, which will lead to more waste, more national debt, more taxes, less economic security, and eventually less national security.

The other issue involving the mainstream media is selectively reporting stories; they suppress the truth and other points of view. The media portrays the Tea Party as a right wing militia group capable of extreme violence. They ignore the already known violence committed by the left because it does not suit their political agenda. They portray anyone who doesn't agree with them as extremists and dangerous in order to diminish their viewpoints or their voice. This does not allow for a free exchange of ideas and can prevent the American public from having the information or facts they need to form their own opinions.

The worst part is that the media has a tremendous influence on certain segments of the population. They have the power to influence the most vulnerable of our population and advance their agenda or cause. For example, the media made former vice-president Al Gore appear like a rock star. His attempt to influence Americans about global warming with An Inconvenient Truth made him wealthy, and influenced many young people to believe his science. However, the media ignored the fact that all of his statements were conjectures made on assumptions that were not yet scientifically proven. This created a manufactured global warming crisis, which may have been part of an agenda to bring the democratic nations in the world toward a more socialistic and green approach to world climate, and/or make Al Gore rich. The media conveniently ignored all sides of the issue from the scientific front that were in opposition and conveniently failed to note the hypocrisy of Mr. Gore making a lot of money while using more non-green energy than the average citizen.

Let's not forget that the mainstream media overtly supports president Obama and his policies. They are not looking out for the majority of American interests. The media's support of Obama's health care legislation as well as all the Democrats that voted for it does not protect Americans. At the expense of benefiting 10 to 20 percent of Americans initially, the health care bill will hurt more than 80 percent of people by increasing their cost and decreasing their access to care. This will cause lower quality of care and higher death rates for Americans. The media is no longer our watch dog.

Therefore, one should not vote for candidates supported by the mainstream media; this is why they are on the "who not to vote for" list.

Chapter 7

Teachers

When discussing teachers, I am mainly referring to those in the public sector who are employed by government. Many teachers in the public sector have jobs that are protected by their unions and this creates an atmosphere of non-accountability. The majority of teachers want to do well and make a difference. There are some wonderful teachers that have had a positive impact on students' lives. But the nature of the profession, with the government paying their salary and the unions making it practically impossible for them to be fired, causes them to be naturally protective of government. After all, the security of their jobs is at stake. This results in a tendency to support big government, reducing the value of each individual in our nation.

Because of this relationship with big government, they are not suitable candidates on the whole. It is generally believed that teachers are greater than 80 percent to the left of center, usually voting democratic or are at least registered Democrats. As we know, Democrats in general believe that government is more likely the solution than the problem. Democrats want to make government bigger and have more control over the individual. We as a nation are right of center, mainly because of our history and value system. Right of center generally means wanting less government control, more individual rights, more adherence to our constitution, less taxes, and a strong national defense.

Many teachers support big government and, therefore, teach in a way that is influenced by their beliefs rather than facts. For example, many teachers endorse today's green movement (which is good in theory but not proven factually) and teach it to our children. While it is good to learn how to prevent destruction of our planet, the idea that global warming is man made and is caused by carbon emission is, as of today, not proven. The teachers themselves may not understand why teaching children unproven theories of global warming is not appropriate. They believe they are helping future generations, but what they are actually doing is creating a belief system in our children that is not substantiated by facts. They imply the cause of global warming is traced back to Capitalism and big business and that both of these are bad for society. The teachers in essence are telling the children that governments are crucial to preventing or solving these types of problems. These beliefs are subtle disguises of a socialist agenda similar to the European model. What is not taught is that big government is big business and is essentially the biggest business of all.

Teachers take advantage of vulnerable students in their teenage years. During this time, they are often rebellious and tend to disagree with their parents' views. This allows for idealistic views to be more easily accepted. Many young people, especially those that go to college, are extremely vulnerable to liberal arts professors who tend to believe that Capitalism is the root of problems that face our country. It is no wonder why the majority of college students vote as the teachers do. They are not taught enough that liberty, freedom, and success are usually achieved through hard work and sacrifice. Capitalism tends to reward those that work hard and succeed. Many young people are not taught this and choose to follow, as "zombies," the anti-capitalism mantra of their teachers.

Some teachers, through their unions and governments have sweetheart deals. In some states, teachers can retire after twenty years of work and receive most of their yearly salary for life. In

California for example, there are retired teachers and administrators of the board of education who have retired in their fifties receiving close to $100K per year, and are not working. The students may not be so trustful of them if they knew of such sweetheart deals, paid for by the big government they promote. These teachers are benefiting themselves while mortgaging the financial security and future of their own students.

Even more disturbing are the teachers in New York City who are under investigation for either criminal or unprofessional conduct and, instead of being placed on suspension without pay, are placed in "rubber" rooms, receiving their full salary. In what other professions in the private sector would someone receive their full salary while being investigated for possible crimes or misconduct?

Like many of the groups already mentioned, most public school teachers have a reason for wanting bigger government and should not be trusted as potential candidates, nor should we trust the candidates they endorse. Because most teachers are unionized, they will usually vote for their "pocket books." This means even if their views are not completely in line with the candidate, they will vote to preserve their salaries and benefits, meaning, pro big government. Hence, they are on the list of "who not to vote for."

Chapter 8

Other Groups

Other groups that should not get our votes are:

A **People who are not Constitutionalists:** They tend to support judges who interpret the law and legislate from the bench instead of abiding by or following the Constitution. The judicial system, including the Supreme Court, should have people serving it that do not believe the Constitution is one that can be shaped or reformed, but rather believe it to be a document that clearly defines certain inalienable rights that should not be violated by the government. The judges should interpret the Constitution as a form of protection of its citizens from the federal government. The Constitution can only be changed by amendments. Changing the original intent of the framers of the Constitution should not be done. This affects the foundation of our country and ultimately, like a house, may lead to its collapse. Many of today's attorneys, judges, and politicians like the idea of legislating from the bench because this empowers them to more quickly cause social change they believe in and promote. For instance a judge, by a simple ruling, can redefine marriage, whereas an amendment to the Constitution or congressional legislation would be controversial and lengthy. The forefathers did not intend individual judges to have this much power to affect change on controversial social issues that are best left to the legislative branch.

In medicine, for example, one cannot change a certain type of proven treatment because he or she has the power to do so. If a doctor did this, and is wrong, a bad outcome for the patient usually results. The doctor is held accountable and can be sued. However, one who wants to legislate from the bench may not be held accountable for their potential damage of unproven decisions. Many judges today interpret the law according to their personal beliefs. Their decisions regarding public policy or criminal punishment, at times, has resulted in innocent victims being harmed because a judge feels certain groups of people should not be in prison. The O'Reilly Factor featured several segments regarding judges in Vermont who were lenient to convicted child molesters. These judges sentenced child molesters to either community service or short jail sentences, which resulted in further attacks on other innocent children. Using their own sentencing beliefs and power to interpret the law the way they wished, these judges exposed more children to harm.

B People who have worked in Washington, D.C., most of their lives: They tend to see big government as the solution and do not understand how the rest of America lives. Washington, D.C., is the hub of our government, and it suits the own needs of those who have been there a long time to have government as big and as powerful as possible. This benefits them financially because more jobs, and the "perks" that come along with government jobs, will be available to them.

C People who believe in political correctness: In general, they tend to support the minority at the expense of the majority. Just like the latest health care reform bill of March 2010, the intention may be noble in attempting to help cover all Americans with health insurance. But the result is that the majority of Americans suffer right away; and in the long run, almost all Americans will eventually suffer. This is because insuring all Americans without increasing the number of doctors will result in rationing of care and less optimal timely treatment. Also, to contain health care costs, there will be less reimbursement to health care providers, resulting in doctors retiring early, further impacting the rationing of care.

Another example of political correctness involves the mainstream media deliberately choosing not to use the word terrorist or Muslim when a terrorist act is committed on our citizens by a Muslim extremist. This occurred with both the Muslim psychiatrist at Ft. Hood, who killed soldiers, and the Muslim terrorist who tried to blow up a plane over Detroit on Christmas Day, 2009. By being too concerned about offending some Muslims, the press and some political leaders lost sight of the facts of the events and who was really accountable. By not confronting the truth and worrying more about insulting the Muslims, we remain, as a nation, vulnerable to more acts of terrorism against our citizens. The mainstream media, however, can be selectively politically correct. They are quick to point out when Catholic priests have taken advantage of young boys, which all agree is wrong. These pedophile priests should be prosecuted to the full extent of the law, and the Catholic Church should bear some of the responsibility. The press is not concerned it will offend Catholics, and the press shouldn't be concerned how it will affect Catholics, because what the priests did was wrong. Similarly, the press should not be concerned about offending Muslims when Muslim extremists are terrorizing our citizens, because that too is wrong.

D The young and inexperienced: In general, young people tend to be more idealistic, and are not pragmatic. They do not have enough life experiences to understand the full intent of the choices they make. This is why many young people vote with their heart and ideals over acquired knowledge from practical experience. As Winston Churchill is often given credit for saying, "If you're not liberal when you're young, you have no heart. If you're not conservative when you're older, you have no brain." Although more likely quoted by Francois Pierre Guizot, this statement epitomizes the youths' natural progression of idealistic thinking before life makes many of them more practical and realistic.

Teachers and the media influence the majority of the youth, especially those that continue on to college. Many are less influenced by their parents. Many tend to be rebellious to their parents' point of view and are more interested in being contrary than in being complete thinkers. It is hard to be well informed about how government works and how business works when you have not had a steady job or the responsibilities of being independent or providing for a family. Therefore, youths are easy targets for being manipulating into believing that words and ideals will work more than proven methods and results. Youths will one day be the leaders and hopefully, they will refocus their enthusiasm and idealism and will learn to process things pragmatically and factually in order to make more informed decisions, resulting in better governing.

Chapter 9

Comedians in the Democratic Party

Al Franken, I rest my case.

Now that we have learned the process of eliminating certain candidates, we need to think of which categories of people can be most trusted and share most of the values that we would like see in candidates running for office. In other words, "who to vote for."

Section II: __YES__ Votes

Chapter 10

People in Service Industry

People in the service industry, or those who work in areas that serve others, such as health care workers, farmers, construction workers, factory workers, merchants, and all who serve the general public are definitely worthy of receiving your vote. All of these people who serve the public are accountable to their public. Their jobs and success depend on keeping the customer satisfied. They inherently care more about those they serve than do bureaucrats or politicians because their livelihood depends on it (even if it is not during election season).

Service people tend to help others because they want to, not because they have to. Like many parents, and like our founding fathers, they are more willing to make sacrifices to help others because of either their compassion or a pride in doing their work well. The majority of these service people work in the private sector and can be fired for poor performance or sub-standard work performances and are, therefore, more accountable. Generally, when you have more accountability, there is more efficiency and less waste. If the customer is not satisfied, the service person loses that customer. Bureaucratic positions do not have to care if their customers are happy or satisfied; they keep their jobs regardless of customer satisfaction or outcome.

Service people understand that even with hard work and good intentions, bad outcomes can occur, such as lower revenue, resulting in less income and lay-offs. But by using a better approach with proven ways of success and not continuing to use proven ways of failure, the chance for a better outcome and success improves.

For example, doctors are service people who have had to learn that the best way to help others and to be successful in their field is to understand the best approach to take when solving problems. The best approach is scientifically based on results from data that can be reproduced and, therefore, is lacking bias and is unable to be distorted or spun. In my field of cardiology, we assess whether a medication works better than others do by doing studies that involve tens of thousands of people in different medical centers and in different countries. This takes out the possibility of someone fixing the results, is less political, and results in more objective and reproducible data. This data is what ends up helping individual patients as a whole. These studies, when reviewed by experts in the field, result in guidelines that all physicians can follow. These guidelines are updated every few years when newer medications and newer research evolves. The determination of which strategies to use when treating heart attacks is a good example of how these studies ended up improving heart disease by decreasing mortality in our country over the last forty years.

The results of these studies can be trusted because they are based on facts that are reproducible. This raises the question of who do you trust? Many citizens trust their doctors to make good decisions in order to help them with their health problems. This is because they use data substantiated by facts to guide their decision making. They have no political agenda or motivation to do anything other than try to help the patient to their fullest capacity. This is also substantiated by the dedication of people in health care who demonstrate a tremendous work ethic, self sacrifice, and compassion by being willing to be on-call, work holidays and nights, and lose sleep in order to help their patients.

Therefore, in medicine, the outcome determines the guidelines and policy instead of one's opinion. People we vote for should follow this process when governing. In our country, we have historical precedents that are similar to these medical studies. History should count always, not when it is only politically convenient. For example, there are examples of decreasing taxes on Americans and increasing government revenue. This occurred in the 1920s, 1960s, and 1980s, yet, many politicians choose to ignore history and believe that more spending and taxes are necessary when there is a need to increase government revenue.

Physicians and others involved in health care are also accustomed to making tough decisions quickly that may be life or death decisions. Making tough decisions like this under pressure enables one to have a better perspective overall. This qualifies them to be better at addressing less urgent decisions such as political issues. Many times, a physician is confronted with having to make an immediate choice of therapy for patients with heart attacks, trauma, and other emergency situations. They do so relying on their experience and prior training, which is guided by prior proven methods. They have been trained to assess a problem quickly and are accustomed to acting quickly. Their decisions are always based on a strategy that will, in most cases, result in the best outcome. In some cases, good outcomes are not always achievable, such as terminal illness or worsening chronic illness. In these cases, the doctor is able to change course with another set of strategies, treatment options, or recommendations. This is done in order to help the patient realize the reality of their illness and maybe choose a course that will result in more comfort care, but possibly a lessened life span. Politicians too often take sides, but their decisions are based on their party affiliations instead of what is best for the citizens, and many times, they do not change course, even though the known outcome is poor. Politicians would do well to follow the same process and thinking that doctors and other health care workers do, and use methods that have worked in the past and are most likely to work in the future, to help the majority of Americans.

If politicians had utilized the same process of thinking as health care personnel do, they would have approached the latest health care reform bill of 2010 differently. Physicians try to help patients by utilizing successful strategies to treat their illness and incur the least amount of pain possible. Similarly, politicians need to ask the right questions and ask what the desired outcomes are when dealing with health care reform. Asking the right questions in politics is just as necessary as in valid medical studies.

The questions that need to be addressed in the health care reform issue are:

1 Do you want to insure everyone? And who is everyone? Does that include illegal immigrants?

2 Do you want to improve health care? How do you define "improve"? Does insuring everyone actually "improve" the current delivery of health care or does it have the opposite, harming effect?

3 Do you want to decrease the overall cost of health care? Where will the money come from (because if you decrease cost in one sector, you increase cost in another)? Does that mean higher insurance premiums or more taxes or both, or will the government borrow more money and incur more debt?

4 How do insuring all, improving health care quality, and decreasing cost affect each other?

5 Will allowing a free enterprise system for private health care carriers and allowing competition across state lines increase or decrease the overall cost of health care?

6 Will enacting federal guidelines for medical malpractice tort reform and allowing malpractice panels to adjudicate malpractice lawsuits instead of a jury system result in decreased overall health care costs?

Politicians have not addressed these questions in their entirety and, therefore, have left tremendous gaps in trying to reach solutions that could make our health care system more accessible and more affordable. The solutions appear to be more directed toward having more government control of health care and shifting costs from one segment of the population to another segment of the population. That is a redistribution of wealth. Also, these same politicians assure themselves a loyal voting block by giving this entitlement of health care coverage to those who currently do not have health care benefits.

By not addressing the proper questions and not completely dealing with all of the issues regarding health care reform, this incomplete solution or reform law will result, most likely, in the exact opposite of what many well-intentioned politicians may have wanted to achieve. By not fully dealing with all the issues, many more people may become insured, but it will certainly cost the average U.S. citizen more money, and most likely will result in a decrease in the quality of health care.

The reason for the decreased quality of health care is two-fold. One, there will be less money or reimbursement to health care providers and hospitals, and this will result in many health care providers (physicians, PAs, nurse practitioners) leaving the work force. In turn, this will result in less accessibility, meaning it will be harder for patients to see their health care providers because there will be fewer remaining in practice. Two, increasing the number of people insured in our country will also place a strain on the current number of providers. This will result in rationing of care by not being able to see your doctor or health care provider in a timely fashion. In turn, this will result in worse medical outcomes because of the delay in treatment and will naturally cause a decrease in health care quality in the future.

We may have been better served by addressing the problems in health care that were proven to decrease cost by prior experience. Tort reform is known to decrease health care costs nationally, by some estimates over $100 billion. It is known that if health insurance companies were allowed to compete over state lines, it would also lower costs. Car insurance and life insurance compete across state lines and people can choose the type of car or life insurance plan that best suites their needs at a cost they can afford. Americans should be able to do the same with health care plans and have more options and freedom of choice.

Many of the Democrats in Congress in 2009-2010 who supported the latest health care reform bill used their majority control to give the government more control over the health care industry. They used the pretense of helping more American citizens. We know that more Americans will end up with less quality care, more costly care, and more rationing of care. Therefore, the Democrats who voted for this reform should not be voted back into office.

We should be voting for people who have the same values as those in the service industry. Being in politics, and especially in any of the three branches of our government, should be a job of service to the people. They should not be making special deals on the side in order to increase their political power and chance for reelection, and they should not be voting for pay raises and extra benefits secretly in the middle of the night.

Doctors are taught to think of ways to help people by decreasing the odds of bad outcomes. They do this by understanding that all illnesses cannot be eliminated or cured. However, the aim is to continue to find therapies and cures for as many of the illnesses as we can. This process and way of thinking is realistic, in that more patients will die or be harmed if we stopped our research to find newer therapies and cures. Likewise, when it comes to our government protecting our liberty and freedom, such as defending us against terrorism, there needs to be an understanding that terrorism cannot be eliminated. Even if less than 1 percent of 1 percent of Muslims wish our country and its citizens harm, this still will amount to tens of thousands of terrorists wanting to destroy our nation. In medicine, small pox could not be completely eradicated, and many illnesses will never be completely cured; terrorism will not be completely eliminated. Therefore, there has to be a strategy to keep terrorism in check. This can be done by eliminating the terrorists that we know of before they harm us. We try to take care of many illnesses in the same way, by eliminating its cause before it damages our body. The politicians who serve the citizens of this country should think and behave more like physicians caring for their patients. With national security, decisions should always be made to help the majority realizing that there will always be some sacrifices made to preserve freedom and liberty.

Even though these examples involve doctors and health care workers, of which I am most familiar, they apply to all service people. Because most service people understand that being accountable to the public and making sacrifices in their jobs creates the values and principles necessary to be more trustworthy and, therefore, a better candidate. This is why they are on the list of "who to vote for."

Chapter 11

Business Leaders

In general, business leaders are those that run or own either large or small companies or businesses. They generally are entrepreneurs who have taken advantage of the American business model and have succeeded. They understand not only the finances of their business, but have had to work hard and be responsible in order for the business to be successful. Many are self made individuals who started their business from scratch.

Business leaders, especially those that started their own company or business, usually didn't make money the easy way. They have had to work many hours for their money—and are less likely to waste it. They are used to being accountable and responsible because they have many employees who depend on them for providing benefits and paying their salaries. They learn from mistakes and are less likely to make the same mistake in the future because certain mistakes can not only cause a decrease in revenue but can also ruin their business. Similarly, doctors also learn from mistakes in an effort to help their patients better in the future and to avoid lawsuits. When a business leader learns from his or her mistakes, the resultant action usually improves the business both financially and from a quality viewpoint. For instance, if a certain product is losing money, even though the leader feels it is a good product, he/she learns to adapt and change the product until it is successfully marketable.

The qualities of a business leader make them highly qualified for office. They work hard, they have a proven track record of success, they understand being responsible for others, they are willing to make the sacrifices necessary to succeed, and they are more flexible in changing course when something is not working. They are also proven leaders. They are trustworthy because what they do, not what they say, determines the success of their business.

There are business leaders that are less trustworthy. Generally, these tend to be the ones that make money off of other people's hard work or hard earned money. Also, some financial leaders, like investors on Wall Street and big banks, profit by our government not enforcing regulations. Business leaders who have greatly profited by managing other peoples' money are the type of business leaders who should be less trusted if running for office.

The majority of Americans, I believe, do not envy those that make a product that becomes successful and as a result makes them very rich. This is the foundation of American business where being innovative and successful leads to more money in the economy and job growth.

Business leaders who have worked hard and proven to be successful with integrity and honesty are the engine of the American economy that has helped make America the leader of the economic world. This is why they are on the list of "who to vote for."

Chapter 12

The Military

Those retired or enlisted in the military have many of the values that we seek in a candidate. Besides their history of intense training and having a good work ethic, they are dependable, loyal, and brave. They understand the need for sacrifice to help others and their fellow man. They share a belief, like our founding fathers, and a willingness to put their life on the line and lose everything for freedom. Many are heroes and are proven leaders.

The best military leaders worry about their soldiers' welfare. They agonize over decisions to send their troops into battle, knowing it can result in death or serious injuries. They understand the meaning of sacrificing a few for the benefit of many, which is necessary in order to preserve our liberties and freedom. When you understand this, you are an effective leader and are better able to make decisions as a candidate that will benefit most Americans.

There are many examples in the military where a soldier will instinctively put his or her life at risk to save fellow soldiers. For instance, I know of a soldier who was driving a Humvee with four wounded soldiers when he was hit by incoming fire. The gas line on the jeep was leaking, but he took the time to remove all four wounded soldiers out of harms way, without regard to his own personal safety. In less than three minutes, after removing the last wounded soldier from the Humvee, the jeep was engulfed in flames. This soldier demonstrated qualities and values of selfless sacrifice and loyalty not seen in other types of careers. Military personnel have also learned to react quickly in serious situations and do their job well without the need for praise.

The main duty of the military is to protect and serve, which they do selflessly, often leaving their family and country for long periods of time. These personal characteristics of the military enable them to better serve the public in political office. This is why they are on the list of "who to vote for."

Chapter 13

Non-Career Politicians

Non-career politicians are those candidates that do not wish to use politics as a lifelong profession. For reasons that I previously mentioned, candidates that stay in power tend to have more motivation to get reelected than to serve the people. We need to vote for a candidate that pledges to do the following:

1. Vote for term limits, such as no more than twelve years in Congress—whether it is two terms as Senator or six terms in the House of Representatives.

2. Put in writing, such as on the candidate's Web page, his or her positions on all issues. If he/she changes his/her position on an issue at any time, the Web page should be updated with an explanation of why the position changed.

3 Never run as a candidate in one party and then, after being elected, change parties before the term has expired.

4 Pledge to be transparent and mean it. That is, do not give the impression of trying to hide something. All contributions that must be reported should be posted on the candidate's Web site with the name of the donor and the amount given. Also, if a candidate states that TV cameras will be allowed into a discussion of a major form of legislation, such as President Obama's claim to allow C-Span to broadcast the health care reform discussions, and then ignores that promise, he or she should then be questioned by the press until he/she responds as to why he/she didn't fulfill that promise. If the press doesn't do their job, then we need to vote for candidates willing to do the press's job and ask other candidates why they are not fulfilling their promises.

5 Refuse to resort to tactics instead of the normal procedure in passing significant pieces of legislation—like what happened with the final health care reform bill. When it was determined there were not enough votes to pass it in the normal procedure, reconciliation would have been utilized if necessary so that the bill would pass.

6 Hold a fellow member in Congress responsible, who commits misdeeds, even when he or she is in the same party. Also pledge to not use stalling tactics or look the other way so that politicians can remain in office longer because it benefits the party. This requires Congress to be held to the same legal standards as the general population. Congress should be protecting American citizens and not each other, and speak out against any wrong doings by its members.

7 Not add earmarks (pork) to bills and not sneak in self-serving pay raises and extra benefits for him/herself in "late night" legislation.

8 Not character assassinate someone who disagrees with his or her position. There needs to be some degree of civility.

9 Let the public see bills in their entirety before voting on them. The public should be allowed to digest it and react to, or comment on, its contents if necessary. No one should buy a house or car, or sign any contract without looking at all the particulars.

And since Congress works for the people, we should be able to see and examine the bills before they sign them into law. Many in Congress should stop acting as if they know better or don't trust the American public.

Candidates who vow to support term limits and actually tell the truth by backing up their campaign promises are a rare breed today. This is why those that do fulfill their pledges are on the list of "who to vote for."

Chapter 14

Those with Faith

Candidates who have faith tend to have more of a service and sacrifice philosophy toward others. Since they have a belief in God, they understand that they are answerable and accountable for their actions here on Earth. They believe that their actions have consequences that affect their lives on Earth as well as their eternal life.

Those with faith usually understand that there is a natural law that all people should adhere to, such as being equal and independent, and existing apart from a political power. Also, no one, including all persons and governments, should harm or take away another person's liberty, health, possessions, or life. Under natural law, all people are born free and have the right to liberty.

Our very country was founded by men who had this philosophy of service and sacrifice. They believed in natural law as a foundation to guide the creation of our government, rules, and laws, which made the government answerable and accountable to its citizens—just as we human beings are accountable and answerable to God.

Many of those who have faith understand that God is like a parent to us. God loves us as all parents love their children. God has given us free will and chosen not to control our actions. Similarly, children also have free will and can choose to do good or bad, regardless of their parents' wishes. Parents are used to sacrificing for their children and love them regardless of their choices in life. Essentially, parenthood is a service industry, as is faith in God, where one puts another's needs ahead of his/her own. Candidates would do well to practice this philosophy.

However, the mainstream press and some politicians are undermining faith and religion. This conveniently makes them less answerable for their actions and less answerable to the truth. Everyone knows that it is wrong to make deals to help oneself at the expense of others, or when involved in legislation, to obtain ones' vote by getting a special individual deal. Yet, there is a rationalization that since politicians are fighting for their own constituents (state or district) it is okay to help some Americans at the expense of others. Candidates who have the values of service, sacrifice, and faith are better suited to see what will help the majority of Americans. They understand that special deals are wrong, even if they help a select few while hurting many others. We are all Americans and must compromise at times; a degree of deal making is necessary in the business of running America. But there needs to be a balance where a smaller group of Americans is not helped at the expense of a larger American group, as we see in the current health care bill of 2010.

Our own founding fathers had many flaws and blemishes, but they had the values that made them great leaders in their time and would make them great candidates in today's world. Our founding fathers generally include those delegates involved in the Declaration of Independence and those delegates involved in our U.S. Constitution. The founding fathers did not have a rampant lust for power as one of their flaws, as British historian, Paul Johnson noted. "These were serious, sensible, undoctrinaire men, gathered together in a pragmatic spirit to do something practical ... [their English political traditions] had always stressed compromise and give and take." Over time, the trapping of power corrupts politicians, as is clearly evident today. They will end up caring about retaining their seats and will do anything not to lose that position. Their reelection becomes more important than helping those they represent. The founding fathers had faith in God, making them accountable for their actions; therefore, the need to obtain and keep power was not one of their main purposes.

The majority of the founding fathers who wrote and signed the Declaration of Independence were religious. There were thirty Episcopalians, twelve Congregationalists, eleven Presbyterians, two Quakers, and one Roman Catholic. Thirty-five of these founding fathers studied law, most of which did not practice law. Seventeen of the founding fathers were either merchants or land speculators. Twelve either owned or managed plantations or farms. Three were physicians, one was a college president, two were small farmers, and Ben Franklin was a scientist, printer, and land speculator. Therefore, the majority of them would have been on the list of "who to vote for."

Today, there are many in the mainstream media that try to undermine religion. They want you to believe that separation of church and state means that the government should not believe in God or in religion per se. As stated earlier, many of our founding fathers were religious and had a strong belief in God. Our government was formed based on both natural law and in a belief or faith in God. In 1813, John Adams, who was our second president, wrote to Thomas Jefferson, "The general principles on which the fathers achieved independence were the general principles of Christianity. I will avow that I then believed, and now believe, that those general principles of Christianity are eternal and immortable as the existence and attributes of God; and that those principles of liberty are as unalterable as human nature." In another letter to Jefferson in 1817, John Adams wrote, "Without religion, this world would be something not fit to be mentioned in polite company, I mean hell."

The people working in government should understand that the government is not God. The government serves the people and the people serve God. Therefore, those with faith understand they are answerable for their actions and are more likely to serve and sacrifice without abusing their power. That is why they are on the list of "who to vote for."

Conclusion

The purpose of this book was to help this nation go back to what once made it great. We should consider the values of candidates that helped make this nation great in the past and can help make it great in the future. This doesn't mean that those on the list of "who not to vote for" do not have these values, but there are more people with these values that will help this nation on the "who to vote for" list. The more a candidate meets these values and flows through the algorithm on page 116, the better the chances our nation is headed in the right direction. The algorithm or flow chart is commonly used by doctors to guide their treatments. You can use the flow chart on page 116 to guide your voting.

Voting is a privilege and should be taken seriously. In our busy lives, we cannot know every candidate in detail. We can, however, make it easier by quickly completing a mental checklist or using a process of eliminating which candidates we should not vote for first. Then we can select a more desirable candidate by determining which one best meets our needs and the country's needs.

When voting, one needs to know who is more trustworthy and has the values such as those that led to the foundation of this country, and then helped the U.S. become the greatest country in the world. The United States represents the nation that allows freedom and liberty for all its citizens more so than any other country. This is because our forefathers had the wisdom to set up a government that was limited and responsible to the people and not the other way around. We are not a great nation because of our government. Our government represents a great nation because of the hard work and values of its people. Our government needs to be run by its people and not by a candidate or that candidate's party.

We can no longer vote for many of the candidates that are in office now, because if they do not support term limits, common sense dictates that they have their own interests at stake more than ours. We deserve more from our elected officials and should expect and demand more.

Since the presidential election of 2008, the government

has grown bigger at a faster rate than ever before. Voting is more important now than it has ever been because people who have a stake in bigger government tend to vote more. That is, government workers vote 75 percent of the time, which is much higher than those in private industry who vote 57 percent of the time and those who are self-employed who vote 61 percent of the time. More people who believe in a smaller government need to vote to offset this higher voter turn out by those who benefit from a bigger government. This is why the congressional elections and presidential elections from 2010 forward will be the most important elections in our generation. We need to make a difference starting with the 2010 congressional elections. When voting, we also need to remember these basic concepts:

1   Stop voting for candidates that say one thing and do another.

2   Vote for candidates for what they did in their life or career and not what they say. Idealism does not govern well; a good track record of success and accountability does.

3 Stop voting for candidates that want to increase the size of government. The government doesn't grow the economy; the private sector does.

Government control tends to hurt the economy through its lack of accountability and through its wasteful practices. The candidates that generally wish for bigger government and a bigger role of government control over the private sector include many of those on the "who not to vote for" list. They do not understand that it is the virtue of government and not the size of government that best fulfills the needs of its citizens.

Government, as our forefathers knew, needs to be smaller and limited. Government needs to be more local, and that is why, initially, the federal government was answerable to the states. After all, spending at the local level instead of at the federal level is more efficient and results in better and less costly services. One needs not to forget that the U.S. government is the biggest business. It has become more corrupt and less accountable than any other business. Many times, its members do not follow the rules that it enforces on its own citizens. Let us make them accountable and vote only for those candidates representing the values we believe in.

If you believe that government is good, should be in charge of your life, and knows what is best for you, then keep voting for the same politicians. Many of these politicians want more control and power. They get these by making government bigger. This will only benefit them while hurting many of us, our children, and our grandchildren.

If you believe that you should be the one to determine what is best for our country and that the government represents you, then you need to exercise your right to vote by voting intelligently. That is, vote for candidates that have the values of proven trustworthiness, those that have lived a life of sacrificing for fellow man, those that have succeeded in their business, and those who have and practice faith.

At times, one will still need to vote for the lesser of two evils; this could represent a candidate you disagree with on some issues, but is still close to you on most of your beliefs. By not voting, it is possible that a weaker and less desirable candidate will win, and potentially cause more harm. Also, please use your common sense and life experiences, and don't continue to vote for candidates that generally help themselves more than the citizens they represent, or those that believe bigger government is the solution to your problems.

Do we want to continue this progressive movement that began one-hundred years ago leading this nation toward more federal government control, more taxes and debt, and less individual rights and freedoms? This progressive movement is endorsed by the mainstream media, progressive teachers who are influencing our youth, and the politicians, attorneys, union leaders, lobbyists, and bureaucrats who are helping to continue this massive spending agenda and government take-over. Or do we want to reclaim this country by having government answer to us and be both financially responsible and protect our individual liberties? By voting more often for those on the list of "who to vote for," we stand the best chance of moving the country in a healthier direction where we the people are again in charge as our forefathers always intended.

Life Support Flow-Chart for Voting to Save This Country

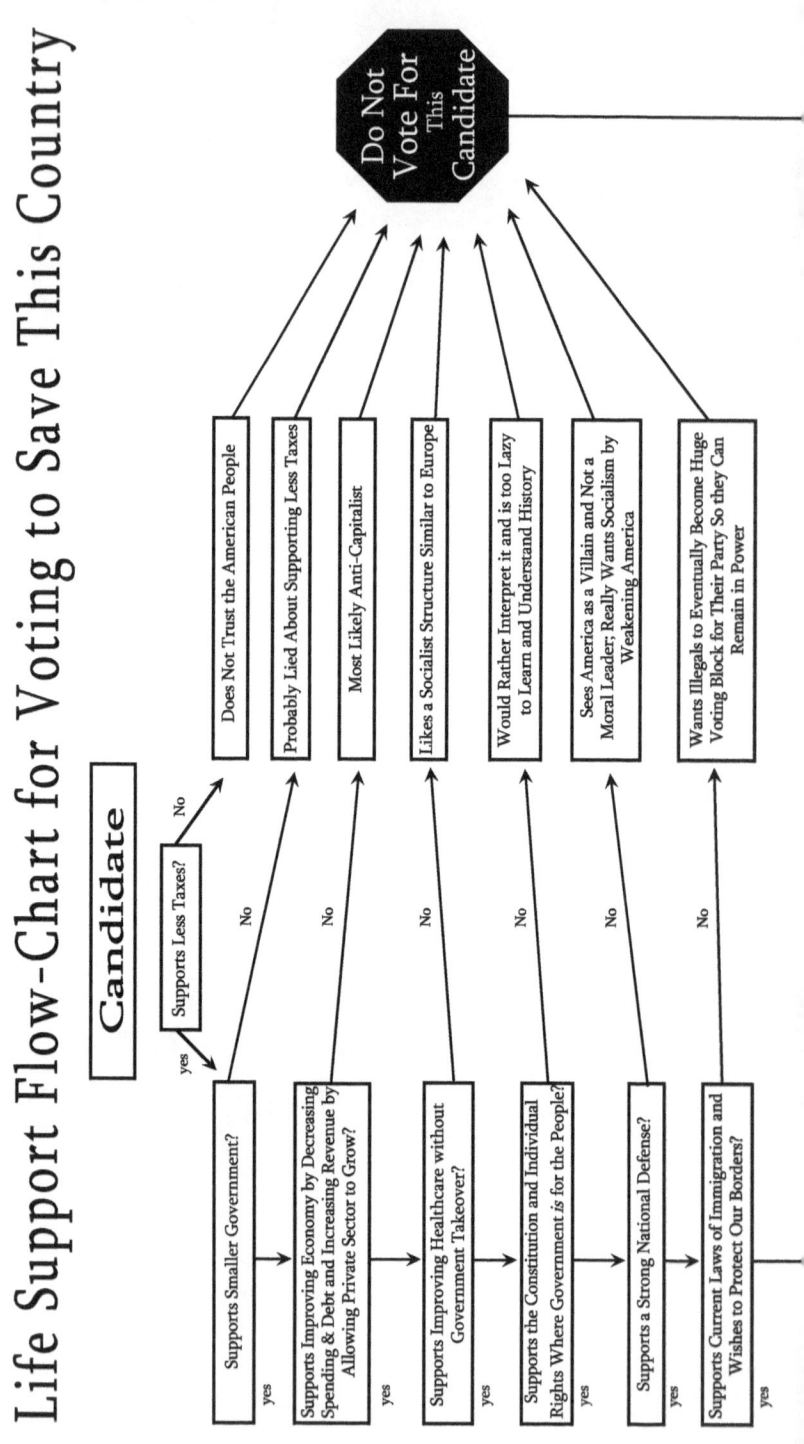

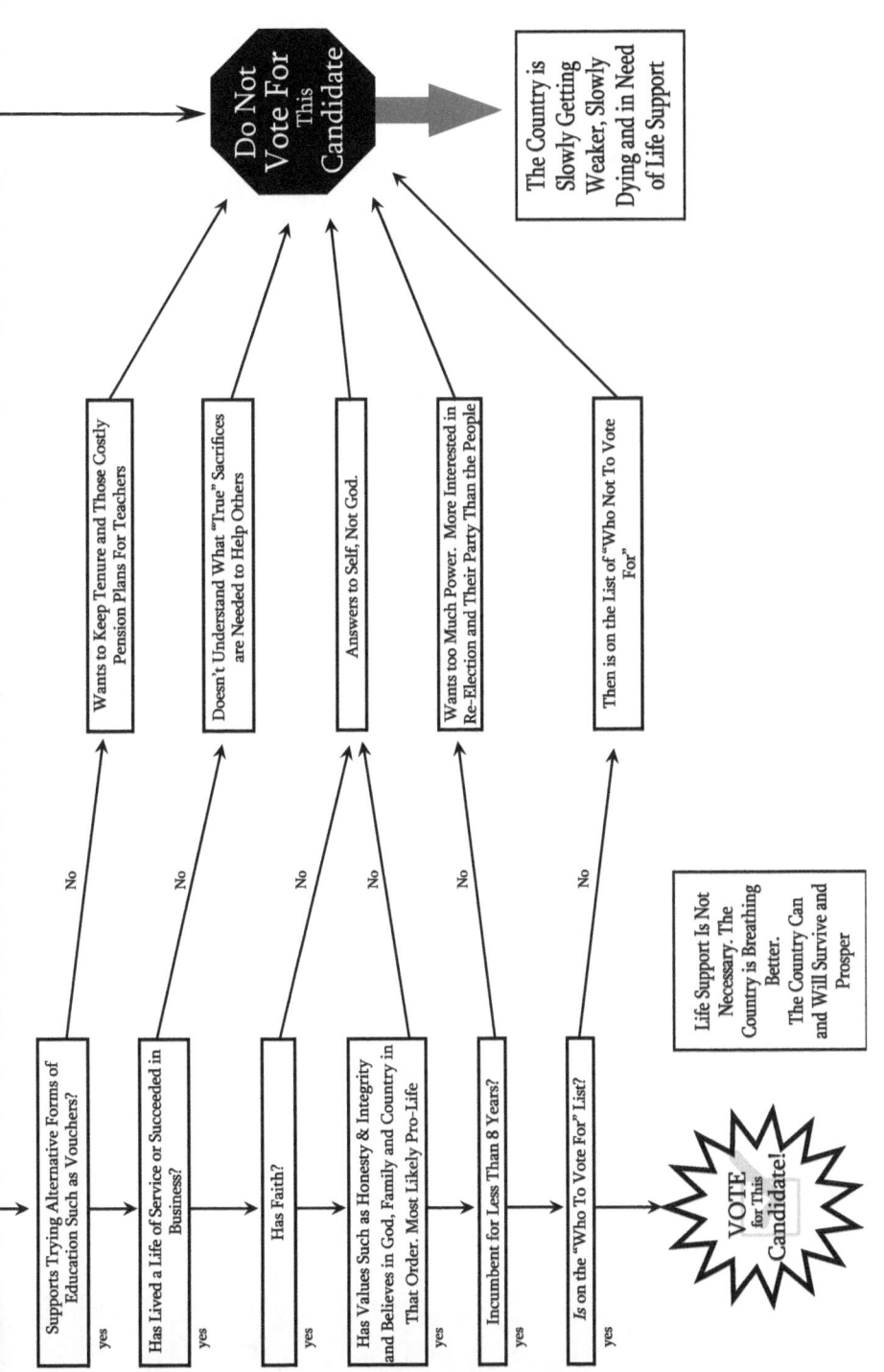

SOURCES

Bader, Hans. "Overpaid Bureaucrats Expand in Number and Pay." OpenMarket.org. September 30, 2009. http://www.openmarket.org/2009/09/30/overpaid-bureau crats-expand-in-number-and-pay/.

Center for Responsive Politics, Revolving Door. "Reelection Rates Over the Years, (1964-2008)." OpenSecrets.org. http://www. opensecrets.org/bigpicture/ reelect.php (accessed May 15, 2010).

Churchill Centre and Museum at the Cabinet War Rooms, London. "Myths". http://www. winstonchurchill.org/learn/myths/ myths/ quotes-falsely-attributed-to-him (accessed May 16, 2010).

Chrysler Labor Talks, 2007. Economic Data. Auburn Hills, Michigan. April 2010. http://www.chryslerLabortalks.com/Economic_ Data.pdf (accessed May 3, 2010).

Coco, A., D. Cohen, M. Horst, & A. Gambler. "Trends in Prenatal

Cares Settings: Association with Medical Liability." Research Institute & Department of Family and Community Medicine, Lancaster, PA, July 22, 2009. http://www.biomedcentral com/1471-2458/9/257 (accessed May 2, 2010).

"Doctors Moving to States with Malpractice Caps." Daily News Cetral, June 1, 2005. (no author) http://health.dailynewscentral.com /content/view/925/ (accessed May 22, 2010).

Daily, Paul. "List of Lawyers in the 111th Congress." Liberty Forum. http://www.dailypaul.com/node/94514 (accessed May 28, 2009)

Dolan, Kerry. "The Drug Research War." Forbes, May 28, 2004. http:// www.forbes.com/2004/05/28/cz_kd_0528 outsourcing.html (accessed May 2, 2010).

Encyclopedia Britannica. "François Guizot." http://www. britannica. com/EBchecked/topic/249050/Francois-Guizot (accessed May 13, 2010).

Fix It Together.Org. "Term Limits Amendment, Summary of our Pro posed Amendment," http://fixittogether.org/ index.php?option =com_content&view=article&id=60:term-limits&catid=38:am endments&Itemid=58 (accessed April 30, 2010).

Gonzalez, Jose. "Texas' Medical Liability Landscape Improves After Tort Reform Enacted." American Academy of Pediatrics News 31, 5 (2010): 20.

Hope & Humor James Watkins.com. "Were United States Founding
    Fathers Christians?" July 2003. http://www.jameswatkins.com/
    founingfathers.htm (accessed April 25, 2010).

Johnson, Paul. A History of the American People. New York: Harper
    Perennial, 1997.

Mattera, Jason. Obama Zombies: How the Liberal Machine Brain
    washed My Generation. New York: Threshold Editions/
    Simons & Schuster, 2010.

Nano, Stephanie. "Study: Malpractice Worries Help Drive Health
    Costs," Associated Press, April 13, 2010. http://www.google.
    com/hostednews/ap/article/ALeqM5g1X8n7Ct5xyKui-jeaw4J
    VS8AXYwD9F2DTP81 (accessed May 25, 2010).

Napolitano, Andrew. The Constitution in Exile: How the Federal Gov
    ernment Has Seized Power by Rewriting the Supreme Law of
    the Land. Nashville, TN: Thomas Nelson, Inc., 2006.

O'Reilly, Bill. "Journalists, Liberalism and Education." The O'Reilly
    Factor, January 3, 2006. http://www.billoreilly .com/show?acti
    on=viewTVShowByDate&date=20060103(accessed May 2,
    2010).

O'Reilly, Bill. "Investigating the NEA." The O'Reilly Factor, May 10,
    2006. http://www.billoreilly.com/ show?action=viewTVShowB
    yDate&date=20060510 (accessed May 2, 2010).

Rizo, Chris. "Texas Legal Environment Improves, Survey Shows." The Southeast Texas Record, March 22, 2010. http://www.setexas record.com/news/225475-texas-legal-environment-improves-survey-shows.

Schweikart, Larry and Michael Allen. A Patriot's History of the United States. New York: Sentinel/Penguin Group, 2007.

U.S. Bureau of the Census. Voting and Registration, November 2008.

U.S. National Archives and Records Administration. Executive Orders Disposition Tables John F. Kennedy – 1962. www.archives.gov /federal-register/executive-orders/1962.html (accessed May 20, 2010).